Mary Jones, Diane Fellowes-Freeman
and David Sang

Cambridge Checkpoint
Science

Workbook
8

CAMBRIDGE
UNIVERSITY PRESS

CAMBRIDGE
UNIVERSITY PRESS

University Printing House, Cambridge CB2 8BS, United Kingdom

One Liberty Plaza, 20th Floor, New York, NY 10006, USA

477 Williamstown Road, Port Melbourne, VIC 3207, Australia

314–321, 3rd Floor, Plot 3, Splendor Forum, Jasola District Centre, New Delhi – 110025, India

79 Anson Road, #06–04/06, Singapore 079906

Cambridge University Press is part of the University of Cambridge.

It furthers the University's mission by disseminating knowledge in the pursuit of education, learning and research at the highest international levels of excellence.

www.cambridge.org
Information on this title: www.cambridge.org/9781107679610

© Cambridge University Press 2012

First published 2012

40 39 38 37 36 35 34 33 32 31 30 29 28 27 26 25

Printed in India by Repro India Ltd

A catalogue record for this publication is available from the British Library

ISBN 978-1-1107-67961-0 Paperback

Introduction

What is this workbook for?

This workbook will help you to develop your knowledge and skills in science.

As you work carefully through it, you should find that you get gradually better and better at doing things such as:

- using your knowledge to work out the answers to questions, rather than just remembering the answers
- organising, displaying and using data from secondary sources
- planning experiments, recording results, drawing graphs and making conclusions.

How is the workbook organised?

The workbook exercises are arranged in the same order as the topics in your coursebook.

Each exercise has the same number as a topic in the coursebook.

There is not always an exercise for each topic. For example, there is an exercise for each of topics 1.1, 1.2, 1.3 and 1.4. There is no specific exercise for topic 1.5.

The exercises will help you to develop the skills you need to do well in science.

The exercises are not quite the same as the questions that you will meet in the Progression Tests or your Checkpoint examination. This is because the exercises are to help you to get better at doing particular things, rather than testing how well you can do them.

Contents

Physics

Unit 1 Plants

Exercise 1.1   The beginning of photosynthesis

This exercise will remind you about how we can use rocks to find out what happened long ago. You will also need to think about what is produced by photosynthesis.

The chart shows some important events that occurred during the very early history of the Earth.

1500 million years ago
The first, very simple animal-like organisms appeared.

3000 million years ago
The first organisms that could photosynthesise appeared.

4000 million years ago
Living organisms first appeared on Earth.

4600 million years ago
The Earth was first formed.

1 How long after the formation of Earth did the first life appear?

....

2 Suggest how we know when the different kinds of organisms first appeared on Earth.

....

....

....

....

3 Up to about 3000 million years ago, there was no oxygen in the Earth's atmosphere. Today, about one fifth of the atmosphere is oxygen gas.

Use the information on page **6** to suggest what caused this change.

....

....

....

....

4 Suggest why animal-like organisms did not appear on Earth until after the first organisms that could photosynthesise had appeared.

....

....

....

....

 **Unit 1** Plants

Exercise 1.2   Drawing leaves

> You don't need to be a good artist to be able to make good scientific drawings. This exercise will help you to learn some of the important things to think about when you are drawing a biological specimen.

Choose an interesting leaf. In the space provided below, make a large, labelled drawing of the upper surface of the leaf.

Before you start, read through the checklist on the next page. When you have completed your drawing, give yourself a mark out of three for each statement.

Checklist

0 = I didn't even try

1 = I tried, but didn't do very well

2 = I did quite well

3 = I did really well

Statement	Mark out of 3
I used a sharp pencil for my drawing.	
I used a good eraser and completely erased all the mistakes I made.	
I did not use any colour or shading on my drawing.	
I made my drawing bigger than the actual leaf.	
The shape and proportions of my drawing are exactly like those of the leaf.	
I showed the edges of the leaf very clearly.	
I showed the pattern of veins on the leaf very clearly.	
I labelled at least three things on my drawing.	
I used a ruler to draw the labelling lines.	
I made sure the end of each labelling line touched the part of the leaf I was labelling.	
I wrote the labels around the drawing, not on top of it.	
Total (maximum possible mark = 33)	

Exercise 1.3 The effect of different colours of light on the rate of photosynthesis

Sunil wanted to find out which colour of light would make a plant photosynthesise fastest.

The diagram shows the apparatus that he set up.

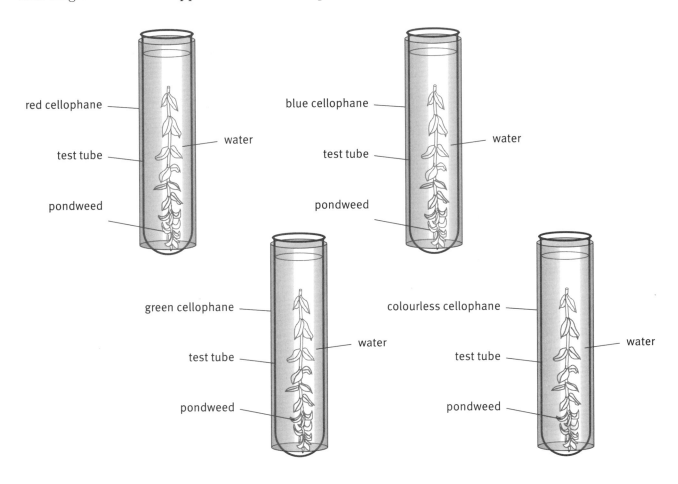

Sunil shone a light onto each piece of pondweed. He counted the number of bubbles that was given off in one minute. He did this three times for each piece of pondweed.

These are his results.

red – 10, 12, 11   blue – 8, 12, 10

green – 4, 5, 6   colourless – 11, 13, 12

1 What was the variable that Sunil changed in his experiment?

....

2 What was the variable that Sunil measured in his experiment?

....

3 List **three** variables that Sunil should have kept the same in his experiment.

first variable ....

second variable ....

third variable ....

4 Draw a results table in the space below, and fill in Sunil's results so that they are easy to understand. Remember to include a column where you can write in the mean value for each set of results.

5 Complete the bar chart to show Sunil's results.

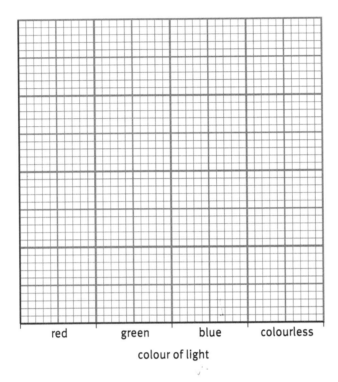

red   green   blue   colourless

colour of light

6 Write down a conclusion that Sunil can make from his results.

....

....

....

Exercise 1.4 Plants in space – Extension

You will need to use both your own knowledge and the information in the box to answer these questions. Some of the questions will make you think back to topics that you learnt about last year – gravity and soil.

Read the information, and then answer the questions that follow.

The International Space Station has been orbiting the Earth since the year 2000. More than 200 astronauts, from many different countries, have worked on the Space Station.

Some of the astronauts carry out experiments to investigate how plants grow in space. The plants are grown in small, enclosed, transparent containers. They are given artificial light. Air and water are pumped around their roots.

The experiments show that, when there is no gravity at all, the plant roots and shoots grow randomly in all directions. So some of the plants are spun gently in a machine called a centrifuge. This produces a force to which the plants respond just as they would respond to gravity.

One experiment has tested how the plants grow in different kinds of soils. If a soil has very large particles, the water in it escapes easily. The water forms little droplets and floats away into the air. If the particles in the soil are very small, then air does not flow through it easily and the roots don't get enough oxygen to survive.

The plants grown in the Space Station include dwarf wheat, strawberries and mizuna. If humans ever travel to Mars, they will need plants to provide them with oxygen and food. The experiments also show that the astronauts enjoy growing the plants.

1 Suggest why the plants in the Space Station are grown in enclosed containers.

....

....

2 Suggest why water has to be pumped directly to the plant roots, rather than just poured into the container from a watering can.

....

....

Unit 1 Plants

3 a Explain why the roots of a plant grow in all directions if there is no gravity.

....

....

b Describe how this problem has been solved in the Space Station.

....

....

4 Explain why a sandy soil would not be a good choice for growing plants in the Space Station. (Use what you know about soils, and also the information on page **13**, to help you write your answer.)

....

....

....

....

5 Describe **three** reasons why it would be useful for astronauts travelling on a long journey to grow plants in their spaceship.

first reason ....

....

second reason ....

....

third reason ....

....

Unit 2 Food and digestion

Exercise 2.1   Fibre in food

This exercise asks you to use data in a table, and to look for a particular pattern in the data. You'll also practise drawing a bar chart.

The table shows the fibre content of some different foods.

Food	Grams of dietary fibre per 100 g of food
apples	2
bananas	3
beans	5
bread, brown	7
bread, white	4
chicken	0
coconut	14
corn	4
eggs	0
fish	0
fries (potato chips)	2
mutton	0
peas	5
plantain	6
potatoes	3
rice	3
spinach	6
sweet potatoes	2
yam	4

1 Explain why we need fibre in our food.

....

....

2 Which kinds of food do **not** contain any fibre?

....

3 Calculate the total amount of fibre there would be in a meal containing 200 g of chicken, 200 g of rice and 100 g of spinach. Show your working.

....

4 Choose any **ten** of the foods in the table, and draw a bar chart to show how much fibre they contain. Think about a sensible order in which to arrange the different foods in your bar chart. Remember to label each axis fully.

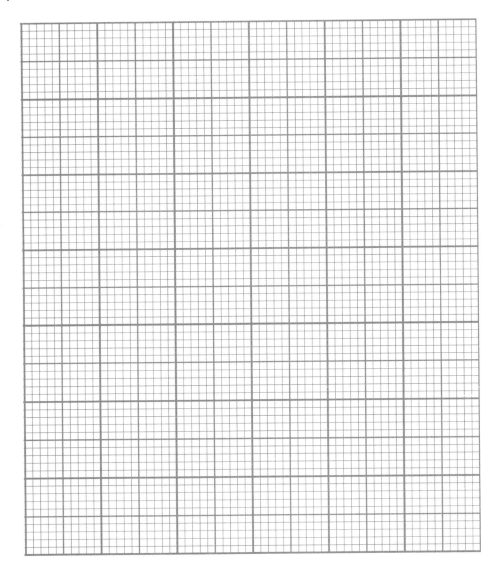

Exercise 2.2 Energy requirements

> In this exercise, you will practise finding information in a written passage, and in a bar chart. Make sure that you write the answers in your own words – don't just copy sentences from the passage.

Read the information, and then answer the questions.

> The cells in your body are always using energy. All of their energy comes from the nutrients in the food that you eat – especially from carbohydrate and fat. Cells can also get energy from protein.
>
> If you eat too much of these nutrients, your cells do not use all of the energy from them. Your body turns the extra nutrients into fat. The fat is stored, mostly just below the skin.
>
> If you don't eat enough of these nutrients to provide all the energy your cells need, the cells have to find another source of energy. They break down the body's fat stores to provide energy. You lose weight.
>
> Different people need different amounts of energy each day. In general, men use more energy than women. People who have active lives use more energy than people who spend a lot of time sitting down.

1 Which **two** nutrients provide most of the energy for the cells in the body?

....

2 A man eats food containing more energy than he uses up each day. What will happen to his weight? Explain your answer.

....

....

3 The bar chart shows the average energy needs of six different groups of people.

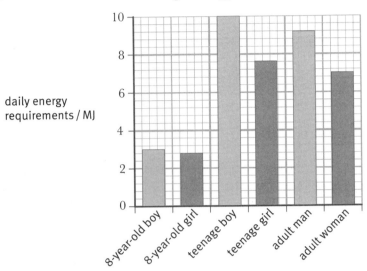

a What are the average daily energy needs of an eight-year-old girl?

....

b Approximately how much energy should an eight-year-old girl take in (as food) each day?

....

c Suggest why most eight-year-old boys need less energy each day than a teenage boy.

....

....

....

....

d Suggest why, on average, an adult woman needs less energy each day than an adult man.

....

....

....

....

Exercise 2.3   Digestion

This exercise will help you to think about the exact meanings of several of the words associated with diet and digestion.

Write clues for this crossword.

¹a	b	s	o	r	²p	t	i	o	n

Crossword grid:

¹absorp(2)tion across
1-down: alimentary (a-l-i-m-e-n-t-a-r-y)
2-down: protein (p-r-o-t-e-i-n)
³molecule
4-down: digest (d-i-g-e-s-t)
5-down: starch (s-t-a-r-c-h)
6-down: sugar (s-u-g-a-r)
⁷nutrient
⁸anus
⁹amino
¹⁰iodine

Across

1 ....

....

3 ....

....

7 ....

....

8 ....

....

9 ....

....

10 ....

....

Down

1 ....

....

2 ....

....

4 ....

....

5 ....

....

6 ....

....

Exercise 2.4   Functions of the digestive system

There's a diagram showing the different organs in the digestive system on page **24** in your coursebook. Their functions are described on page **25**. This exercise will help you to learn the position of each organ, and to link each organ to its function.

Decide which organ carries out each of the functions in the list below.

Then use a ruler to draw a label line to the organ in the diagram, and label its function. You could write in the name of the organ, too, if you like.

You will need to write in some of the functions more than once, because they are carried out by more than one organ.

Functions
- makes pancreatic juice
- produces hydrochloric acid
- protein is digested here
- starch is digested here
- fat is digested here
- saliva is produced here

- small molecules of nutrients are absorbed through the walls
- water is absorbed through the walls
- makes bile
- stores bile
- food is chewed into smaller pieces

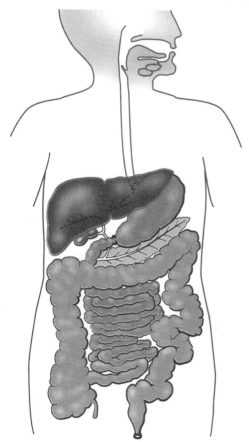

Exercise 2.6   How do teeth help in digestion?

> This exercise gives you practice in planning an investigation. It will also
> help you to think about how teeth and enzymes each have a part to play in
> digestion. You may be able to carry out your investigation after your teacher
> has checked it. If so, do make improvements to it if you think of any while you
> are working.

We use our teeth to break food up into smaller pieces. This helps enzymes to get at
all parts of the food, so they can break the large molecules into small molecules.

Plan an investigation to answer this question:

> Does chewing food help amylase to break down the starch in bread faster?

You don't need to actually chew the bread. You can just break it up into smaller
pieces.

1 Which variable will you change in your investigation?

....

2 How will you change this variable?

....

....

3 Which variables will you keep the same?

....

....

....

....

4 How will you measure how quickly the amylase breaks down the starch?

....

....

....

....

....

....

....

....

5 How will you record your results? Draw a results table that you could use.

6 Predict the results you would expect. Explain why you would expect this to happen.

....

....

....

....

Unit 3 The circulatory system

Exercise 3.1   Blood flow in the human circulatory system

This exercise will help you to remember how the human circulatory system works. The diagram is not quite the same as the one in the coursebook, so you will have to think about it. Remember to take care when drawing labels – use a ruler to draw label lines and make sure the end of the line is in exactly the right place.

The diagram on the opposite page shows a plan of the human circulatory system.

1 Draw an arrow inside each of the four blood vessels that connect with the heart, showing which way the blood flows inside them.

2 Draw **two** arrows inside the heart – one on each side – to show how the blood flows through it. Your arrows can be curved if you wish.

3 Label each of these parts:

   lungs

   artery carrying blood to the lungs

   vein carrying blood from the lungs

   kidneys

   artery carrying blood to the kidneys

   vein carrying blood from the kidneys

4 Use a red pencil to lightly shade all the parts that contain oxygenated blood.

5 Use a blue pencil to lightly shade all the parts that contain deoxygenated blood.

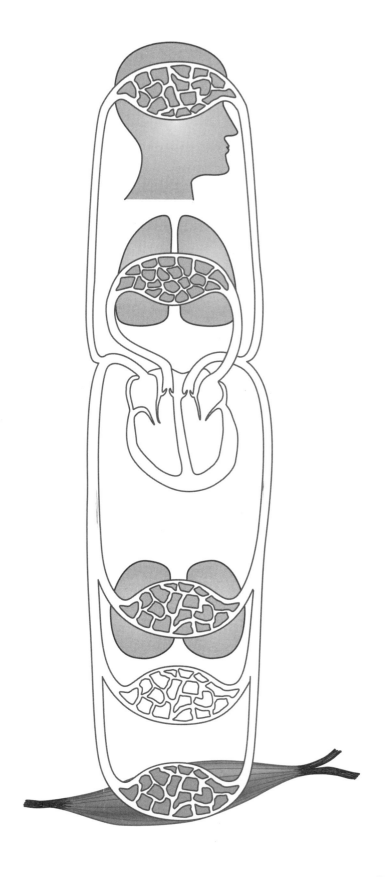

Exercise 3.2 **Hummingbirds**

Data that you have not collected yourself is said to be a secondary source. In this exercise, you will practise organising, displaying and interpreting data from a secondary source. You will also practise looking for correlations in data.

Hummingbirds are very small and very active birds. They feed on nectar, which they collect by inserting their beaks into flowers as they hover.

Scientists measured the body masses of ten hummingbirds. They also measured the mass of the heart of each hummingbird. These are their results.

hummingbird 1	body mass 2.2 g, heart mass 0.05 g
hummingbird 2	body mass 7.5 g, heart mass 0.13 g
hummingbird 3	body mass 9.8 g, heart mass 0.18 g
hummingbird 4	body mass 6.2 g, heart mass 0.14 g
hummingbird 5	body mass 7.8 g, heart mass 0.16 g
hummingbird 6	body mass 3.5 g, heart mass 0.06 g
hummingbird 7	body mass 12.0 g, heart mass 0.23 g
hummingbird 8	body mass 4.2 g, heart mass 0.10 g
hummingbird 9	body mass 9.5 g, heart mass 0.15 g
hummingbird 10	body mass 5.8 g, heart mass 0.13 g

1 Record these results in a table in the space below. Think about the best order in which to arrange the results. Remember to give clear headings to the columns or rows.

2 Draw a line graph to show these results. Put body mass on the *x*-axis (the one along the bottom). Put heart mass on the *y*-axis (the one up the side). Draw a best fit line through your plotted points.

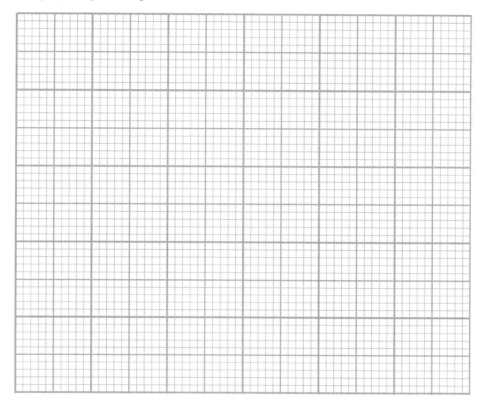

3 The scientists concluded that there is a correlation between the body mass of a hummingbird and the mass of its heart. (A 'correlation' means that there is a relationship between the two masses.) Explain how their results provide evidence for their conclusion.

....

....

....

4 Suggest a reason for the relationship between the body mass and heart mass of a hummingbird.

....

....

Exercise 3.3   Adapting to high altitude – Extension

> Do you know the altitude at which you live? This exercise asks you to think
> hard about how the human body can make changes to allow a person to live
> even at very high altitudes, where oxygen is in short supply. You will need to
> link together information given in writing, information given in two graphs, and
> also your own knowledge. Not easy!

There is much less oxygen in the air at high altitudes than there is at low altitudes.
When a person moves quickly from a low altitude to a high altitude, they may
get out of breath very quickly and feel ill. This is because they cannot get enough
oxygen into their blood.

However, if they move upwards more gradually, their body has time to respond to
the change by making more red blood cells.

A party of trekkers wanted to walk from Phakding to Everest Base Camp in
Nepal. They planned their trek carefully, to give their bodies time to adjust to the
changes in altitude. The graph shows their plan.

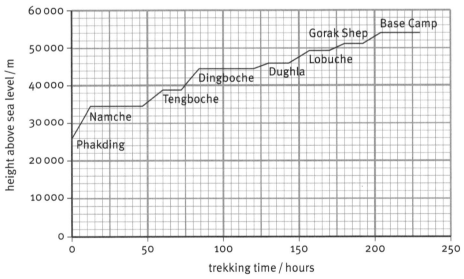

1 How many days did the trekkers predict it would take them to walk from
   Phakding to Everest Base Camp?

....

2 What is the altitude at Namche?

....

3 How long did the trekkers plan to stay at Namche?

....

4 Suggest why they planned to stay at Namche and Tengboche for several days, before continuing to climb upwards.

....

....

One of the trekkers was a doctor. She took blood samples from herself and the other trekkers during their trek. She measured the amount of oxygen in the blood. The graph shows the results.

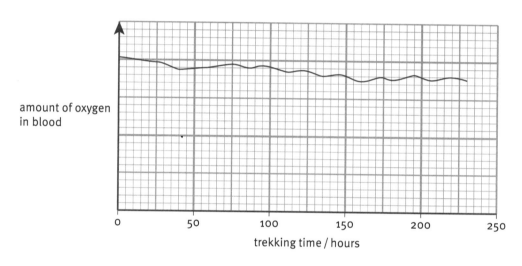

5 Explain why the amount of oxygen in the trekkers' blood decreased during the trek.

....

....

....

6 If a person travels quickly from Phakding to Everest Base Camp, the amount of oxygen in their blood becomes so low that they may become very ill. Explain why this did not happen to the trekkers.

....

....

....

....

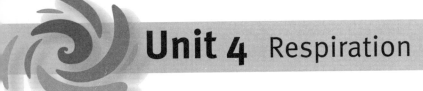

Unit 4 Respiration

Exercise 4.1 A model of the human respiratory system

You may be able to make or use a model like the one described in this exercise. Thinking hard about how it works will help you to understand how breathing movements make air move into and out of the lungs. You will need to use what you know about gas pressure, which is explained on pages **76** to **77** in the coursebook.

The diagram shows a simple model of the human respiratory system.

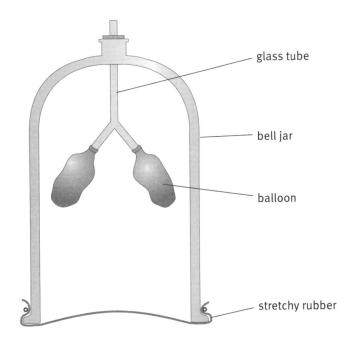

glass tube

bell jar

balloon

stretchy rubber

1 Suggest which parts of the model represent each of these parts of the body.

the lungs ....

the diaphragm ....

the trachea ....

the rib cage ....

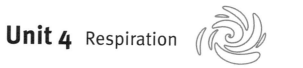

2 a What happens to the space inside the bell jar when the stretchy rubber is pulled downwards?

....

b Complete this sentence about gas pressure:

The more space a gas has, the .... its pressure is.

c What happens to the pressure of the air inside the bell jar when the stretchy rubber is pulled downwards?

....

3 When the stretchy rubber is pulled downwards, the balloons inflate.

Here is some more information about gases and pressure:

- The pressure of the air **outside** the bell jar does not change when the stretchy rubber is pulled downwards.

- Gases flow from a high pressure area to a low pressure area.

Use this information, and your answers to **2a**, **b** and **c**, to explain why the balloons inflate when the stretchy rubber is pulled downwards.

....

....

....

....

....

....

Exercise 4.2   Lung surface area and body mass

> This exercise provides you with data about six different mammals. You will practise looking for correlations in data, and suggesting explanations for the patterns that you find.

The table shows the body mass of six mammals. It also shows the total surface area of the air sacs in their lungs.

Mammal	Body mass / g	Total surface area of air sacs / m²
human	80 000	70
mouse	20	0.1
rabbit	4 000	8
rat	300	0.8
sheep	68 000	60
fox	20 000	40

1   The entries in the table are not in a very helpful order.

Complete the table below by reorganising the entries in a way that makes it easier to see any patterns in the data.

2 Describe the relationship between body mass and total surface area of the air sacs.

....

....

....

3 Suggest an explanation for the relationship you have described.

....

....

....

Exercise 4.3 An investigation using hydrogencarbonate indicator

You have probably used limewater to test for carbon dioxide. In this exercise, you will learn about another way to test for this gas, using an indicator. You will also need to use your skills in planning investigations, thinking about variables, using results to make conclusions and making predictions.

Hydrogencarbonate indicator changes colour according to how much carbon dioxide there is in it.

- The indicator is purple when there is no carbon dioxide.
- The indicator is red when there is a low concentration of carbon dioxide.
- The indicator is yellow when there is a high concentration of carbon dioxide.

Kushi set up four boiling tubes like this:

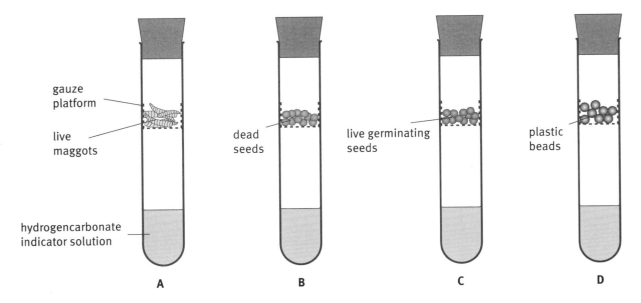

Kushi recorded the colour of the indicator in each tube at the start of her experiment. Then she left the tubes in the laboratory for two hours, and recorded the colour again.

This is what she wrote down.

A red   yellow   B red   red

C red   yellow   D red   red

1 Suggest why Kushi used a gauze platform in each tube.

....

....

2 Suggest why Kushi put a bung in each tube.

....

....

3 Describe **two** variables that Kushi kept the same in her experiment.

....

....

4 Construct a results table in the space below, and complete it to show Kushi's results.

5 Explain Kushi's results.

....

....

....

....

....

....

....

....

....

6 a Predict the result that Kushi would obtain if she set up another tube containing some little living green plants.

....

....

b Explain your prediction.

....

....

....

7 Plan an experiment, using the apparatus that Kushi used, to find the answer to this question:

Do bean seeds respire faster than pea seeds?

Remember to think about the variable you will change, the variables you will keep constant, and the variable you will measure.

....

....

....

....

....

....

....

....

....

....

....

....

....

....

....

....

Exercise 4.4   Recording breathing rate and depth

> People who are keen on keeping fit often like to measure their breathing rates when they are exercising. In this exercise, you will work out some values from a slightly different kind of graph than you have used before. Once you have found these values, you will try to explain them.

Pietro used a machine to measure his breathing rate. He breathed in and out of the machine. The machine recorded the volume of air he breathed in and out with each breath, for one minute.

Pietro collected a set of results when he was sitting still, and another set when he was running on the spot.

Then he printed out the results that the machine recorded. This is what they looked like:

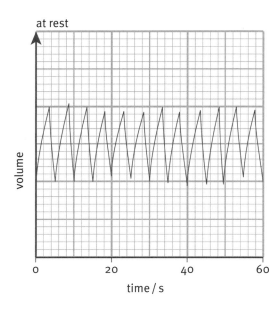

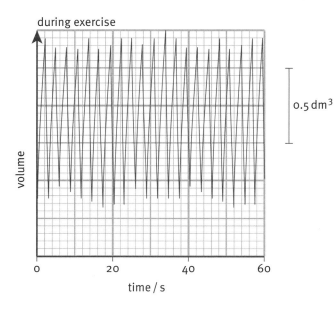

1 How many breaths did Pietro take in one minute when he was resting?

....

2 a Use the graph to work out the volumes of air breathed in with each of the first ten breaths that Pietro took when he was resting. Write them down.

....

....

b Calculate the mean volume of these ten breaths.

....

3 How many breaths did Pietro take in one minute when he was running?

....

4 a Use the graph to work out the volumes of air breathed in with each of the first ten breaths that Pietro took when he was running. Write them down.

....

....

b Calculate the mean volume of these ten breaths.

....

5 Explain the reasons for the differences in Pietro's breathing when he was resting and when he was running.

....

....

....

....

....

Unit 4 Respiration

Exercise 4.5 Smoking statistics

> In this exericise, you will practise displaying a set of data as a bar chart. First, though, you will try to find some data for yourself, using the internet. You will then need to think about the labels for the axes of your bar chart, the scales that you will use and how to draw the bars. Once you have drawn your bar chart, you will use it to help you to answer some questions.

The table shows the percentage of women and men who were smokers in ten countries in 2009.

Country	Percentage of women who were smokers	Percentage of men who were smokers
Russian Federation	24	58
Chile	32	38
Indonesia	5	61
Netherlands	27	31
China	2	51
Maldives	11	42
Egypt	1	40
Pakistan	6	33
India	3	46
Nigeria	4	10

1 If your country is not listed in the table, use the internet to find the data for it.

If your country is listed, find data for another country that you are interested in.

Country ....

Percentage of women who smoked ....

Percentage of men who smoked ....

2 On the grid below, construct a bar chart to display the data in the table, and the other data that you have found.

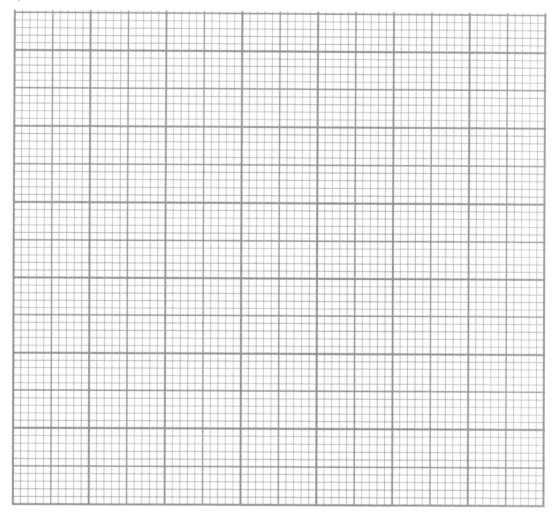

3 **a** In which country did the greatest percentage of women smoke in 2009?

....

   b In which country did the greatest percentage of men smoke in 2009?

....

   c In which country was there the biggest difference in the percentage of women who smoked, and the percentage of men who smoked?

....

Unit 5 Reproduction and development

Exercise 5.1 External fertilisation

> This exercise involves using new information, and what you have already learnt, to work out the answers to questions. You will also think about how different animals are adapted to reproduce in different ways.

Read the information below, and then answer the questions that follow.

In mammals, including humans, fertilisation happens inside the body. A sperm cell fuses with an egg cell inside the oviduct. This is called internal fertilisation.

In most amphibians and fish, fertilisation happens outside the body. The female lays her eggs in water. Then the male adds sperm cells to them. The sperm cells swim through the water, find the eggs and fertilise them.

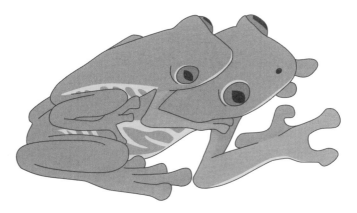

Amphibians, such as tree frogs, have to go back to water to breed. Tree frogs often lay their eggs in little pools of water that are trapped in holes in trees, or in bromeliad plants.

1 Explain the meaning of the term **fertilisation**.

....

....

2 Explain the difference between **internal fertilisation** and **external fertilisation**.

....

....

....

3 External fertilisation can only happen in water. Suggest why.

....

....

4 Most animals that have external fertilisation produce more eggs than animals that have internal fertilisation. For example, humans produce only one egg cell at a time. Fish produce thousands of eggs at a time.

Suggest some reasons for this.

....

....

....

....

Exercise 5.3   The menstrual cycle

This exercise gives you practice in interpreting information provided in a graph.

1 Draw one line from each word to join it to its definition.

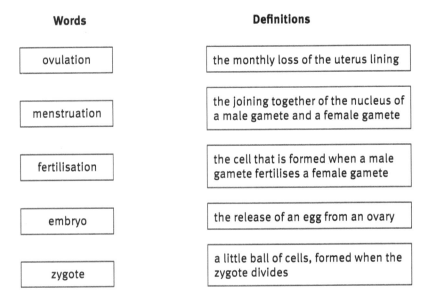

Words	Definitions
ovulation	the monthly loss of the uterus lining
menstruation	the joining together of the nucleus of a male gamete and a female gamete
fertilisation	the cell that is formed when a male gamete fertilises a female gamete
embryo	the release of an egg from an ovary
zygote	a little ball of cells, formed when the zygote divides

The graph shows how the lining of the uterus changes during one menstrual cycle.

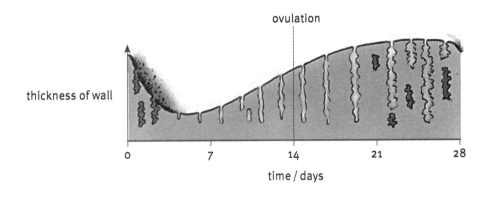

2 How many weeks does the menstrual cycle shown in the graph last?

....

3 The first day of the cycle was on 1st June. On which date did ovulation happen?

....

4 On which of these dates could fertilisation happen? Circle the correct answer.

    1st June   **12th June**   **15th June**

5 Explain why it is important for the lining of the uterus to start to get thicker before ovulation happens.

....

....

....

Exercise 5.4 Gestation periods

In this exercise, you will practise organising data in the best way. You will also think about the meaning of the word 'correlation', and practise using data to support an argument.

The **gestation period** of a mammal is the time between fertilisation and the birth of a baby animal. It is the time during which the young animal develops inside the mother's uterus.

The table shows the mean mass of an adult female of eight different species of mammal, and the mean gestation period for that species.

Species	Mean mass of a female / kg	Mean gestation period / days
moose (elk)	550	245
llama	113	330
goat	15	150
wolf	40	64
lion	150	108
rabbit	1	33
elephant	5000	640
chimpanzee	40	227

1 In the table below, rearrange the data so that it is easier to see if there is a relationship between the mean mass of a female and the mean gestation time.

Species	Mean mass of a female / kg	Mean gestation period / days

2 Is there a correlation between the mean mass of a female and the mean gestation time? Explain your answer, and use figures from the table to support it.

....

....

....

....

....

3 Suggest why the figures in the table are shown as 'Mean mass' and 'Mean gestation time', rather than simply 'Mass' and 'Gestation time'.

....

....

....

Exercise 5.5   Human growth

> This exercise gives you practice in reading graphs. You will have to think carefully about how you can work out the rate from a graph. The rate of growth is how quickly size changes over time. So you will need to look at the steepness of the line on the graph to answer the questions about rate.

The graph shows the mean heights of boys and girls of different ages.

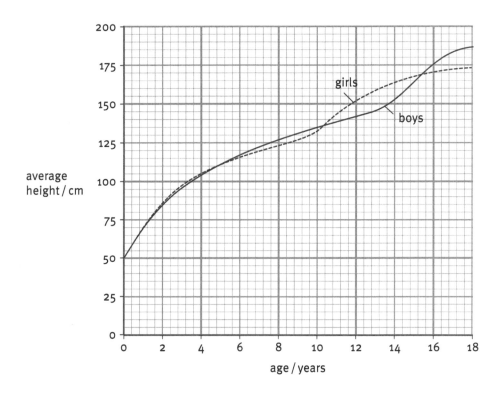

1 What is the mean height of boys at age 12?

....

2 Between what ages is the mean height of girls greater than the mean height of boys?

....

3 Between which of the following ages is the **rate** of growth of boys the greatest? Circle the correct answer.

    0–2 years   **4–6 years**   **16–18 years**

4 There is a growth spurt – that is, the rate of growth increases – at puberty. Use the graph to suggest when puberty happens

in girls ....

in boys ....

Exercise 5.6   Does caffeine affect birthweight?

In this exercise, you will look at some data collected by researchers in Sweden. You will practise using data to make conclusions, and thinking about how an investigation could be improved.

A study was carried out in Sweden to investigate the idea that women who drink a lot of coffee during pregnancy might have smaller babies. 1037 pregnant women took part. They each answered a questionnaire about how much coffee they drank.

When their babies were born, their birthweights were measured. The results are shown in the table.

Mean caffeine intake per day /mg	Mean birthweight / g
less than 100	3660
100 to 299	3661
300 to 499	3597
500 or more	3694

1 Plot these results as a bar chart on the grid. Think carefully about the range for the scale on the y-axis. Remember that you do not need to begin at 0.

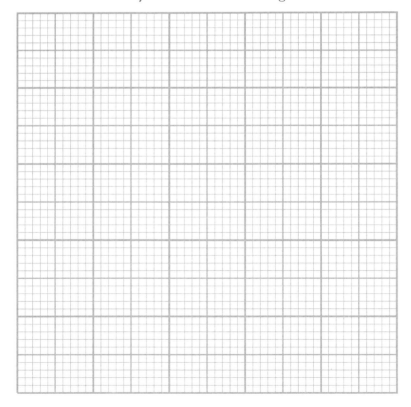

Unit 5 Reproduction and development

2 What conclusion can you make from these results? Explain your answer, and use figures from the table to support it.

....

....

....

....

....

3 Suggest **two** ways in which the researchers could have improved their study.

....

....

....

....

Exercise 6.1 Particle theory

This exercise will help you to understand and remember particle theory.
Remember that 'explaining' something means that you have to say not only
what happens, but also **how** or **why** it happens. Explaining is more difficult
than describing!

1 In the boxes below, draw diagrams to show how the particles are arranged in
a solid, a liquid and a gas. Remember that all the particles should be the same
size.

Solid	Liquid	Gas

2 Explain, in terms of particle theory, what happens when ice is heated and melts
to form water.

....

....

....

3 When the solid iron bar in the diagram is heated, it no longer fits the holder.

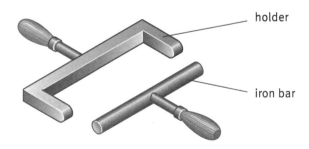

holder

iron bar

Use particle theory to explain why this happens.

....

....

....

4 Use the terms below to match the statements below. Each word may be used
once, more than once or not at all.

boil	**compressed**	**condensation**	**evaporation**
freeze	**gas**	**heat**	**liquid**	**melting**	**move**
solid	**vibrate**		

a A state of matter where the particles do not touch each other:

....

b When a gas is cooled to form a liquid: ....

c Particles in a solid do this: ....

d Solid changing to a liquid: ....

e When a liquid changes into a gas: ....

f The particles in liquids and gases can do this: ....

g The state of matter that can be compressed: ....

Unit 6 States of matter

Exercise 6.2 Diffusion

> In this exercise you will use particle theory to explain how diffusion takes place. This exercise will also give you practice in answering questions involving data.

1 When you pass a food stall you can smell what is being cooked. Explain, using particle theory, how this happens.

....

....

....

2 When there is an unpleasant smell in a room, what can you do to get rid of it? Explain why this works, in terms of particle theory.

....

....

....

....

....

3 Marco and Jaden are investigating diffusion. They have 12 Petri dishes filled with agar jelly that has been made up with slightly acidic water and Universal Indicator solution. The jelly is red.

Marco and Jaden have cut circles from the centre of the jelly using a cork borer. They have been given four bottles of sodium hydroxide of different concentrations. The bottles are labelled **A**, **B**, **C** and **D**.

The students place a measured volume of the sodium hydroxide from bottle **A** into the well in the jelly. After 10 minutes they mark and measure how far the sodium hydroxide has diffused into the jelly. They repeat the test twice more.

They do this for the sodium hydroxide from bottles **B**, **C** and **D**.

Here are their results.

Sodium hydroxide	Distance diffused in 10 minutes / cm			
	first attempt	second attempt	third attempt	mean
A	3.2	2.9	3.5	
B	0.7	0.6	0.5	
C	1.5	2.4	2.6	
D	1.6	1.4	1.8	

a   What safety precautions should Marco and Jaden take?

....

....

b   Explain how Marco and Jaden know how far the sodium hydroxide has diffused.

....

....

....

c   Look at the students' results table. Circle any result which you think does not fit the pattern.

d   Complete the table by calculating the mean distances diffused in 10 minutes. (Remember to do the right thing about any result that you think does not fit the pattern.)

e   Which bottle contains the strongest sodium hydroxide? ....

f   Explain how you know this.

....

....

....

Unit 6 States of matter

Exercise 6.3   Investigating diffusion

> In this exercise you will use ideas about diffusion and ideas about investigation skills.

1 You are making tea for some friends. Serena likes her tea very weak, Jose likes his very strong and you prefer yours somewhere in between. Explain, using particle theory, how you make tea for everyone.

....

....

....

....

2 Imagine that you have four food dyes to test, **A**, **B**, **C** and **D**. Imagine that you are going to investigate which food dye diffuses most quickly.

a Which variable will you change? ....

b Which variable will you measure? How will you do this? You can draw a diagram if it helps you to explain.

....

....

c Which variables will you keep the same?

....

....

d How many times will you carry out each test? ....

Explain why you will repeat the tests.

....

....

e How will you know which dye diffuses the most quickly?

....

....

f Draw a results table to show how you would display the results. Fill in the headings of the rows and columns. (Of course, you cannot fill in the rest of the table, because you don't have any results.)

g Why did you choose this way to display the results?

....

....

....

Exercise 6.5   Gas pressure

This exercise will give you the chance to make sure you understand what causes gas pressure.

1 For each sentence, draw a circle round the set of words that correctly completes it.

Gas pressure is caused when particles:

collide with each other

collide with the surfaces around them

Gas pressure increases when particles are:

squashed into a smaller space

allowed to spread out into a larger space

Gas pressure increases when a gas is:

made colder

made hotter

2 Ashraf is at an airport. He has a packet of rice crackers. The packet contains a gas.

Ashraf takes the packet onto an aeroplane. When the aeroplane is high in the sky, the air pressure inside the cabin gets less. The packet inflates.

a   When Ashraf was at the airport, the gas inside the packet was at the **same** pressure as the air around it.

What does this mean? Underline the correct answer.
- Gas particles inside the packet collided with the packet more often than gas particles outside the packet.
- Gas particles inside the packet collided with the packet less often than gas particles outside the packet.
- Gas particles inside the packet collided with the packet just as often as gas particles outside the packet.

b   What changed when Ashraf was in the aeroplane? Underline the correct answer.
- Gas particles outside the packet collided with it less often than they did at the airport.
- Gas particles outside the packet collided with it more often than they did at the airport.

c   Use your answers to **a** and **b** to explain why the packet inflated when Ashraf was in the aeroplane.

....

....

....

....

Exercise 7.1 Atoms

> This exercise will help you to remember the differences between atoms and molecules.

1 Which diagrams show molecules?

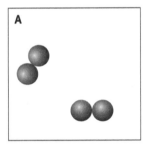 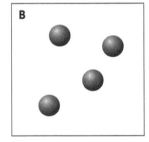 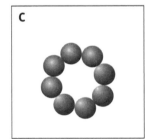

....

2 What can be said about all the atoms in an element?

....

3 Atoms and molecules are both particles. Explain the difference between an atom and a molecule.

....

....

....

4 Draw atoms or molecules in the boxes. Use a circle to represent an atom.

6 individual atoms

4 molecules, each made of 2 atoms

3 molecules each made of 2 atoms, and
2 molecules each made of 4 atoms

Exercise 7.3   The Periodic Table

> This exercise will help you to remember the properties of metals and non-metals and some basic information about the Periodic Table. Questions **3** and **4** will help you to practise using symbols.

1 Write true or false next to each of the following statements.

a   All non-metals are gases.   ....

b   Metals have high melting points.   ....

c   Metals conduct electricity.   ....

d   Non-metals have a dull surface.   ....

e   Non-metals are found on the left side of the Periodic Table.

....

f   In the Periodic Table, a group runs down the table.

....

2 Draw circles around the examples below that are non-metals.

chlorine	silver	helium
carbon	iron	mercury
calcium	neon	sodium
sulfur	gold	zinc

3 Choose the symbols from the list and match them with the names of the elements.

Be   S   K   C   B   Ar   O   Ne   Cl   Ca   H

Name of element	Symbol of element
calcium	
carbon	
oxygen	
beryllium	
hydrogen	
potassium	
neon	
chlorine	

4 Some elements have symbols that do not appear to match their names. For example, the symbol for sodium is Na. Why is this?

....

....

Unit 7 Elements and compounds

Exercise 7.4   Compounds

This exercise will help you to name compounds made from different elements.

1 What is the name of the compound formed when the following elements are combined together?

a iron and chlorine ....

b sodium and oxygen ....

c calcium, carbon and oxygen ....

d hydrogen and fluorine ....

e potassium, nitrogen and oxygen ....

f potassium and nitrogen ....

2 Which elements are found in the following compounds?

a magnesium oxide ....

b carbon dioxide ....

c copper sulfate ....

d calcium chlorate ....

e aluminium chloride ....

f sodium sulfide ....

Exercise 7.5   Using formulae

> This exercise will help you to practise using a compound's name to work out what it contains. You will also practise using a formula to work out not only what the compound contains, but also what its name is.

1   The formula for potassium hydroxide is KOH. Which elements does it contain?

....

2   Which **two** elements do all hydroxides contain?

....

3   The formula for sulfuric acid is H_2SO_4.

   a   Name the **three** elements that sulfuric acid contains.

   1 ....   2 ....

   3 ....

   b   How many atoms of each element are contained in one molecule of sulfuric acid?

....

4   Complete the table.

Chemical name	Formula	What the compound contains
	MgO	
sulfur dioxide		one sulfur atom bonded to two oxygen atoms
aluminium chloride		one aluminium atom bonded to three chlorine atoms
calcium sulfide		one calcium atom bonded to one sulfur atom
	$MgCO_3$	

Unit 8 Mixtures

Exercise 8.1 Mixtures

> This exercise will give you practice in identifying mixtures containing elements and compounds.

The diagrams show particle diagrams.

Use the diagrams in the boxes below to answer the questions.

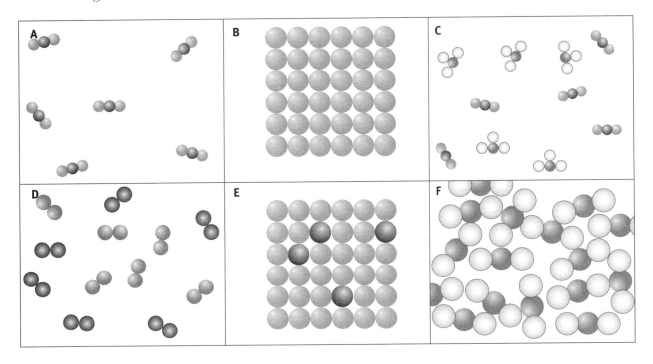

1 Which boxes contain gases?

....

2 Which boxes contain a mixture?

....

3 Which box contains a liquid?

....

4 Which boxes contain a mixture of elements?

....

5 Which box contains a mixture of compounds?

....

Exercise 8.2   More about mixtures

This exercise will give you practice in handling, displaying and interpreting data.

When people talk about gold, you might have heard them say it is 24 carat or 18 carat. What does 'carat' mean? It is a unit to describe how pure the gold is. 24 carat gold is pure gold. If the carat number is lower than 24, then the gold is mixed with another metal – it is an alloy. The other metal is usually silver or copper.

A carat stands for one twenty-fourth. So you can use the unit to work out exactly what proportion of an alloy is gold.

24 carat gold is $24 \times \dfrac{1}{24} = \dfrac{24}{24}$.

It is twenty-four twenty-fourths gold, so it is pure gold.

9 carat gold is $9 \times \dfrac{1}{24} = \dfrac{9}{24}$.

It is nine twenty-fourths gold.

The remaining fifteen twenty-fourths are other metals.

How hard the 'gold' is depends on the amount of gold used and the type of metal used to make the alloy.

An assistant in a jewellery store advises a customer to buy a gold ring that is less than 24 carat. He tells the customer that a ring with a lower proportion of gold looks almost the same as pure gold, but it is harder.

Is this true? The table shows some data on the hardness of 'gold'.

Purity of the gold alloy /carats	Hardness / arbitrary units
9	80
14	90
18	120
22	40
24	30

Unit 8 Mixtures

1 Plot a graph of the information in the table. Take care with the scale on the horizontal axis.

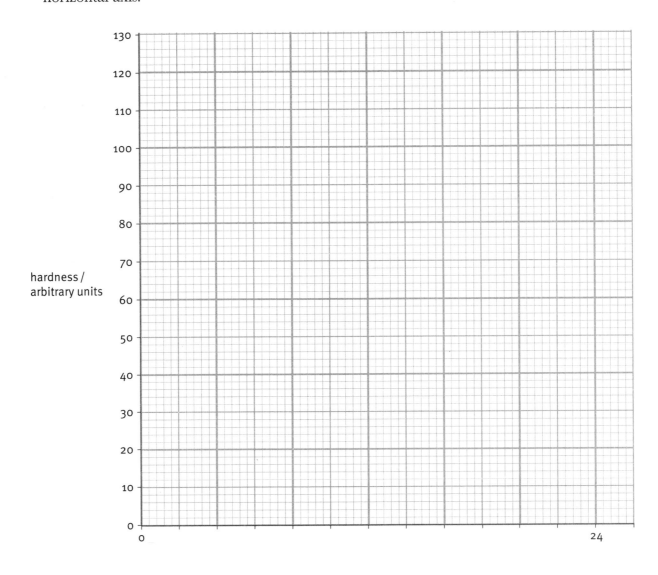

2 Is the advice that the assistant gave the customer based on science or opinion? Explain your answer.

....

....

3 Describe the pattern shown by the graph.

....

....

....

4 You may have expected that the 9 carat gold would be harder than the 14 or 18 carat gold. The data shows that it is not.

Can you suggest why this is so? (Clue – is there another variable, other than the amount of gold in the alloy, that could be affecting the hardness?)

....

....

....

....

Unit 8 Mixtures

Exercise 8.4   Chromatography

This exercise will give you practice in interpreting a chromatogram.

A food scientist is testing the food colouring used in cans of drink. She has to check that any colouring used does not contain any banned chemical.

She places drops of the drink on chromatography paper. She allows the colouring to separate using water.

She also makes another chromatogram, using drops of all the permitted chemical colourings. If she finds anything that does not match with these colourings, she will have to carry out further tests.

The diagrams show her two chromatograms.

chromatogram from the drink

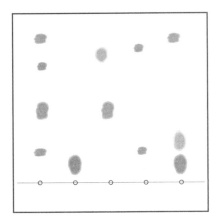

chromatogram of the permitted chemicals

1 Why is the spot of drink placed above the water line at the start of the process?

....

....

2 How many different colourings has the scientist found in the drink?

....

3 Draw a circle around the dye in the drink that is **not** on the permitted list of colourings.

4 Explain why the scientist should carry out further tests on this colouring found in the drink.

....

....

Exercise 8.5   Scientific terms related to solutions

> This exercise will give you practice in using the correct terms involved in this topic.

1 Use the terms given below to label the diagrams. Each term may be used once, more than once or not at all.

dissolves	**evaporates**	**filtrate**	**insoluble**
mixture	**saturated**	**solid**	**solute**
solution	**solvent**	**temperature**	**volume**

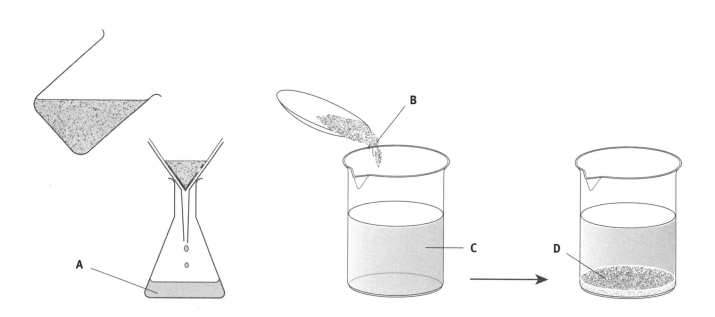

A ....

B ....

C ....

D ....

Exercise 8.6   Solubility

> This exercise will give you practice in working out information from a graph.

The solubility of most solutes increases when the temperature increases. A useful way of showing the different values of the solubility at different temperatures is to plot a graph.

The temperature is plotted along the horizontal axis and the solubility on the vertical axis.

This graph shows the solubilities for copper sulfate, lead nitrate and potassium chloride.

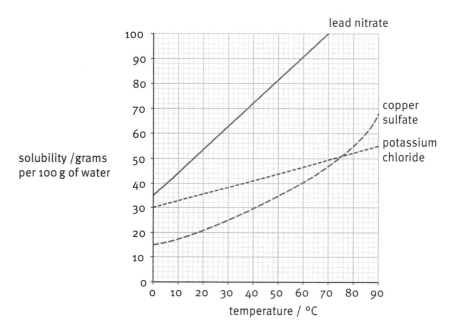

1 What name is given to a solution in which no more solute can be dissolved?

....

2 Explain how you would find the solubility of a solute.

....

....

....

....

3 Why is it important to give the temperature when you state the solubility of a solute?

....

....

4 What is the solubility of lead nitrate at 40 °C?

....

5 What is the solubility of potassium chloride at 20 °C?

....

6 Which of the three solutes is the least soluble at 50 °C?

....

7 Which of the three solutes is the least soluble at 80 °C?

....

8 What is the solubility of potassium chloride and copper sulfate at 75 °C?

....

Unit 8 Mixtures

Exercise 8.7   Solubility investigation

Nadia and Lucy have been investigating the effect of changing the temperature on the solubility of copper sulfate. They used 100 g of water each time.

Here are their results.

Temperature of water / °C	Solubility of copper sulfate / g in 100 g water
10	10
20	15
40	28
60	45
80	67

Here is the graph they produced from their results.

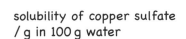

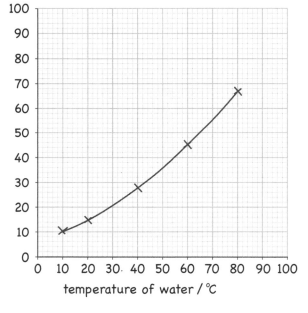

1 What do you notice about the temperatures Nadia and Lucy have used?

....

2 Explain what they could do to improve this.

....

....

....

3 Use the graph to find out the solubility of copper sulfate at 30 °C.

....

4 What could you do to estimate the solubility of copper sulfate at 100 °C?

....

....

5 What do you estimate the solubility of copper sulfate will be at 90 °C?

....

6 What evidence is there that Nadia and Lucy's results are reliable?

....

....

7 Calculate how much copper sulfate would be needed to make a saturated solution of copper sulfate with 400 g of water at 20 °C. Show how you worked this out.

....

....

....

....

Exercise 9.1 Physical and chemical changes

This exercise will give you practice in identifying physical and chemical changes.

1 Give **one** difference between a physical and a chemical change.

....

....

2 Copy the following changes into the correct column in the table below.

ice melting   a wax candle burning

a wax candle melting   toasting bread

mixing the ingredients for a cake   cooking a cake

water boiling and giving off steam

Physical change	Chemical reaction

Exercise 9.3   Reactions with acids

1 When a metal is added to an acid it bubbles and gives off a gas.

   a   What is the name of this gas?

....

   b   Explain how you would test for this gas.

....

....

2 Complete the following word equations:

a | zinc | + | .... acid | → | zinc chloride | + | .... |

b | .... | + | sulfuric acid | → | magnesium sulfate | + | .... |

c | .... carbonate | + | hydrochloric acid | → | copper .... | + | water | + | carbon dioxide |

d | magnesium .... | + | sulfuric acid | → | magnesium sulfate | + | water | + | carbon dioxide |

3 How would you test for the gas carbon dioxide?

....

....

Unit 9 Material changes

Exercise 9.4   Before and after the reaction

This exercise will help you to understand and explain what happens to the atoms in a chemical reaction. It also gives you some practice in using the idea of conservation of mass.

1   The products of a chemical reaction contain the elements calcium, chlorine, hydrogen, oxygen and carbon.

What elements were present in the reactants?

....

....

2   The particle diagram shows the reactants in a chemical reaction.
Complete the word equation and draw a particle diagram for the missing product.

sulfur   +   oxygen $\longrightarrow$ ....

3 This is the word equation for the reaction of magnesium carbonate with hydrochloric acid.

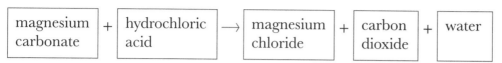

magnesium carbonate + hydrochloric acid → magnesium chloride + carbon dioxide + water

a Which elements are present in magnesium carbonate?

....

b Which elements are present in carbon dioxide?

....

c Water contains the elements oxygen and hydrogen. Where did the hydrogen in the water come from in this reaction?

....

d Where did the chlorine in the magnesium chloride come from in this reaction?

....

4 If the mass of the products of the reaction above was 45 g, what was the mass of the reactants?

....

5 When magnesium reacts with sulfuric acid the products are magnesium sulfate and hydrogen.

If there are 15 g of magnesium at the start of the reaction how much magnesium will be present in the magnesium sulfate?

....

6 Explain what is meant by the term **conservation of mass**.

....

....

Unit 9 Material changes

Exercise 9.5 Explaining unexpected results

This exercise requires you to think about dealing with unexpected results in experiments. It will also help you think a bit more about the idea of conservation of mass.

Marco is investigating the idea of conservation of mass.

- He places some zinc in a beaker and finds the mass of the zinc.
- He places some dilute sulfuric acid in another beaker and finds the mass of the sulfuric acid.
- He then mixes the zinc metal and the acid in another beaker.
- When the reaction has finished, he finds the mass of the contents of the beaker.

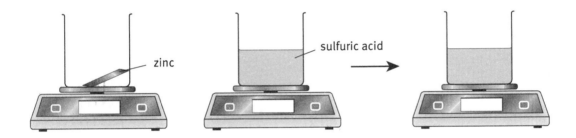

Marco starts with 100 g of zinc and 150 g of sulfuric acid.

1 What is the mass of the products of this reaction?

....

2 Write the word equation for this reaction.

....

3 At the end of the reaction, Marco finds that the mass of the contents of the beaker is 247 g. He repeats the experiment and gets the same result.

a Has he made a mistake?

....

b Suggest why Marco got this result.

....

....

4 When a scientist gets an unexpected result in an experiment what should they do?

....

....

....

Exercise 9.6   Detecting chemical reactions

This exercise will help you to identify when a chemical reaction has taken place. You will also need to use some chemical knowledge that you learnt in earlier units.

1 Give **two** ways you can tell that a chemical reaction has taken place.

....

....

2 Suresh adds some potassium to a beaker of water. The potassium fizzes as a gas is given off.

When the fizzing has stopped, Suresh adds Universal Indicator solution to the water.

a What colour will the Universal Indicator be when it is mixed with the water?

....

b Explain why the Universal Indicator will be this colour.

....

....

c Has a chemical reaction taken place? Explain your answer.

....

....

3 Joanie dissolves some sodium hydroxide in a beaker of water. The pH changes from 7 to 10.

Has a chemical reaction taken place? Explain your answer.

....

....

4 Afua mixes a solution of potassium iodide with a solution of lead nitrate.

Both of the solutions are clear and colourless. The resulting mixture is cloudy and yellow.

a State **two** clues that suggest a reaction has taken place.

....

....

b The yellow precipitate is lead iodide, one of the products in this reaction. What is the name of the other product?

....

c This second product is **not** a precipitate. Suggest where this product is.

....

....

Exercise 9.7   Why does iron rust?

In this exercise you will practise using what you know about why iron goes rusty.

Rusting is a chemical reaction that is not useful.

Surriya is investigating the conditions needed to make iron nails rust. She has set up the experiment as below.

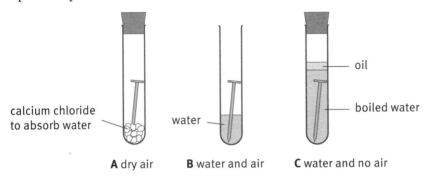

calcium chloride to absorb water

water

oil

boiled water

A dry air   **B** water and air   **C** water and no air

1 What is the chemical name for rust?

....

2 In which tube will the nail go rusty?

....

3 How do the conditions in tube **C** prevent air reaching the iron nail?

....

....

4 In Surriya's experiment she notices that the nail in tube A goes a little rusty.

a   Is this an expected result? ....

b   Suggest how this nail could have rusted.

....

....

5 What could Surriya do to stop a piece of iron from rusting? Suggest **two** ideas.

....

....

6 Plan an experiment to find out if an iron nail rusts more quickly when it is warm than when it is cold.

Remember to think about the variable you will change, the variables you will keep constant, and the variable you will measure.

....

....

....

....

....

....

....

....

....

....

....

....

....

....

....

....

....

Unit 10 Measuring motion

Exercise 10.1 All about movement

These questions will make you think about movement and how we can measure speed.

1 The paragraphs below describe a boy's journey to school.

> Omar wasn't looking forward to school. He walked slowly along the road. Then he heard footsteps behind him. It was his friend Wahid, running to catch up with him.
>
> Together, they walked to the corner of the street to wait for the bus. A car hurried past, throwing up clouds of dust. On the wall nearby, a spider was creeping along. A lizard dashed out and caught the spider.
>
> Omar saw an aircraft flying overhead, leaving a white vapour trail. He thought it would be good to fly so high, or even to zoom off to Mars in a speeding spacecraft.

a In the paragraphs above, draw circles around **all** the words that show that something is moving.

b In the space below, list all the things that are moving, from the fastest to the slowest.

Fastest: ....

Slowest: ....

2 Imagine that you are in a car, driving along a main road.

Along the road, there are signs telling you how far it is to the next town.

At the roadside, there may be marker posts every 100 metres.

Describe how you could use these roadsigns to work out the average speed of the car.

....

....

....

....

....

....

....

....

....

....

Exercise 10.3   Calculations involving speed

This exercise will give you practice in calculating speed, distance and time. Take care with units. Speed may be in m/s or km/h.

1 A bird flies 75 m in 15 s. Calculate its speed.

....

2 A bus travels from one city to another, a distance of 80 km. It takes 1.6 hours. Calculate its average speed on the journey.

....

3 A spider runs along the top of a wall at a speed of 0.24 m/s. How far will it run in 5 s?

....

4 An advertisement for a new car states that its top speed is 180 km/h. If it could travel at this speed for 3 h, how far would it go?

....

5 Ahab has been sent to the shops by his mother. The shops are 1200 m from his home. If Ahab can run at an average speed of 6 m/s, how long will it take him to reach the shops?

....

6 A Japanese bullet train can travel at 300 km/h. How long will it take to cover a section of track 180 km in length?

....

7 The table shows the World Records for male sprinters in 2011 over different distances. Complete the table by calculating the average speed of each runner.

Distance in metres	Time in seconds	Speed in m / s
100	9.58	
200	19.19	
400	43.18	

Over which distance do sprinters have the greatest average speed?

....

8 A robber is in a fast car, hurrying away from the scene of his crime. His car can go at 150 km/h. He will be safe if he can reach the border, 40 km away.

A police car arrives at the scene of the crime. The police are late! The robber has already travelled 10 km towards the border. The police car sets off in hot pursuit.

a   How far is the robber from the border at this time?

....

b   Calculate how long it will take the robber to reach the border.

....

c   How fast must the police car travel if it is to catch the robber before he reaches the border?

....

Unit 10 Measuring motion

Exercise 10.4   Patterns of movement

> These questions will help you to understand how an object's movement can be represented in different ways.

1 a A ticker timer can show the pattern of movement of an object. The timer marks a dot on the tape 50 times each second. The tape below was made by pulling it at a steady speed through the timer. The dots on the tape are evenly spaced.

On the blank tape shown below, draw the pattern of dots you would expect to see for an object moving at a faster, steady speed.

b The tape below was attached to an object that was speeding up. The dots on the tape get farther apart as the object goes faster.

On the blank tape shown below, draw the pattern of dots you would expect to see for an object that was slowing down. (Mark the 'start' point on the tape.)

c On the blank tape shown below, draw the pattern of dots you would expect to see for an object that speeds up and then moves at a steady speed. (Mark the 'start' point on the tape.)

2 Three distance/time graphs are sketched below.

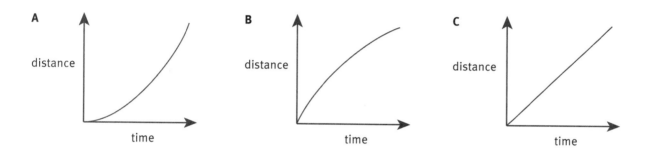

a Which graph (**A**, **B** or **C**) represents the movement of an object whose speed is decreasing?

....

b Look at the distance/time graph below. It shows the movement of a car travelling at constant speed along a road. Add a second line to represent the motion of another car which is also travelling at constant speed, but more slowly than the first car.

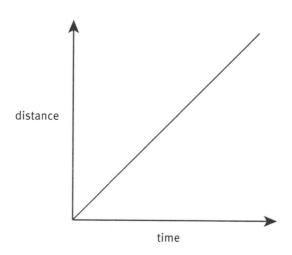

3 A railway timetable can provide information which can be turned into a distance/time graph. The timetable below shows some of the stopping points of the Himchal Express, a train that runs northwards from Delhi to Himchal in India.

Station	Departure time	Distance in km	Time since departure in minutes
Delhi	22:45	0	0
Sonipat	23:52	44	67
Samalkha	00:14	72	89
Karnal	01:06	123	
Ambala City	03:14	205	
Morinda	04:38	275	
Ghanauli	05:30	308	
Nangal Dam	07:15	355	
Una Himchal	07:50 (arrival)	371	

a Complete the last column to show the time since departure from Dehli.

b Use the information to draw a distance/time graph for this journey.

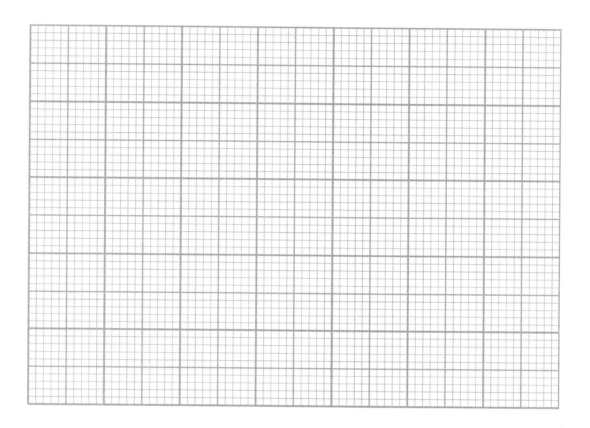

c Calculate the average speed of the Himchal Express.

Exercise 10.5   All in a graph

> This exercise illustrates how much information you can extract from a distance/time graph.

The graph below (also shown in your coursebook) represents a cyclist's journey up a hill and down the other side.

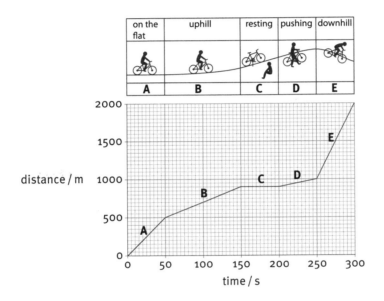

1   In section **A** of the journey, the graph is a straight line sloping upwards. This shows that the cyclist is moving at a steady speed.

   a   How far does the cyclist travel during section **A**? ....

   b   How long does section **A** take? ....

   c   Calculate the cyclist's speed during section **A**.

....

2 These questions are about section **B** of the journey.

a How can you tell from the graph that the cyclist is travelling at a steady speed?

....

....

b How can you tell from the graph that the cyclist is travelling more slowly than in section **A**?

....

....

c Why is the cyclist travelling more slowly?

....

....

d Calculate the cyclist's speed during section **B**.

....

3 This question is about section **C** of the journey.

How can you tell from the graph that the cyclist is stationary (not moving)?

....

....

4 These questions are about section **E** of the journey.

   a How can you tell from the graph that this is the fastest section of the journey?

....

....

   b Why is the cyclist travelling most quickly in this section?

....

....

   c Calculate the cyclist's speed during section **E**.

....

5 Put the sections of the journey in order, from slowest to fastest:

Slowest				Fastest
C				E

Exercise 11.1   Making music

> This exercise will help you to understand how different sounds can be
> produced using musical instruments.

Musicians can play many different notes on their instruments. They can play loud
notes and soft notes. They can play high-pitched notes and low-pitched notes.

Your task is to interview a musician about how they play their instrument. (You
may be able to answer the questions for yourself if you play an instrument.)

Fill in the spaces below with answers from your interview.

1 a   Name of instrument ....

b   Name of musician ....

c   Type of instrument (stringed, wind, percussion) ....

2 How can the musician change the loudness of a note?

....

....

....

....

....

....

3 How can the musician change the pitch of a note? Explain what changes can produce a note with a higher pitch.

....

....

....

....

....

....

Exercise 11.3   The speed of sound

In this exercise, you will interpret information about the speed of sound.

How fast does sound travel? When someone speaks to you, you can hear what they say almost as soon as they start speaking.

It's a bit different if you see a lightning strike. The thunder and lightning are produced at the same time. However, you see the flash first. A little later, you hear the thunder. This shows that sound (thunder) travels more slowly than light (the flash of lightning).

1 The picture shows an experiment to measure the speed of sound. The person with the timer starts it when he sees the smoke from the starting pistol and stops it when he hears the bang.

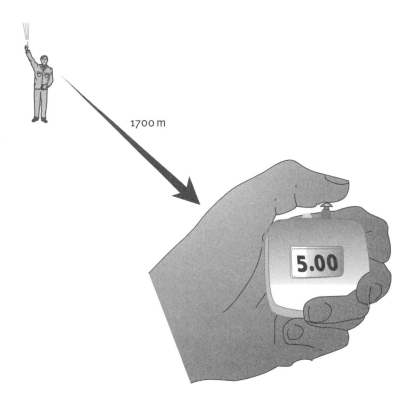

1700 m

5.00

The timer shows 5.0 s when the person stops it.

a Use the information in the picture on page **101** to calculate the speed of sound in air.

Distance travelled by sound = ...

Time taken = ...

Speed of sound in air =

....

b How far would sound travel at this speed in 10 s?

....

c Do you think this is an accurate way to measure the speed of sound in air? Explain your answer.

....

....

....

2 The table shows the speed of sound in different substances.

Material	Speed of sound in m/s
air	330
water	1500
concrete	3000
steel	5000

a   Does sound travel faster in steel or in water? ....

b   Sound travels twice as fast in concrete as in water. True or false?

     ....

c   Whales call to each other when they are underwater. Their calls can travel
     very long distances. How long will it take for a whale call to reach another
     whale at a distance of 60 km?

     ....

Unit 11 Sound

Exercise 11.4   Louder and louder

> In this exercise, you will interpret data concerning the loudness of sounds.

Our ears can hear a great range of sounds, from very soft to very loud. The loudness of a sound is measured on a scale called the decibel scale. The decibel (dB) is the unit of loudness.

The diagram below shows the scale and shows some typical sources of sounds with their loudnesses.

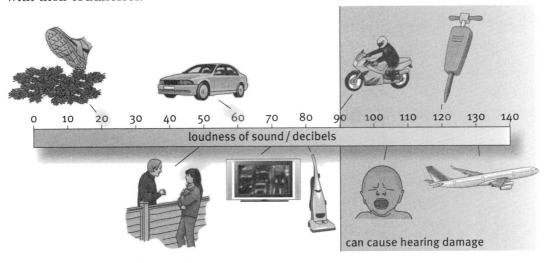

loudness of sound / decibels

can cause hearing damage

Answer these questions, based on the diagram.

1 Which end of the scale (left or right) has the loudest sounds?

....

2 Which is louder, a car or a motorbike?

....

3 According to the diagram, what is the loudness of a television set?

....

4 The diagram shows that the loudness of a conversation is about 50 dB. Do you think that all conversations have the same loudness? Explain your answer.

....

....

....

5 Loud sounds can damage your hearing. Could a crying baby cause damage? Explain how you can tell from the diagram.

....

....

6 Explain why people who work at an airport may have to wear ear protectors.

....

....

7 Sounds louder than 90 dB can damage hearing. Young people can damage their hearing by listening to music that is too loud. They may do this by turning up the volume of their headphones, or by standing by the loudspeakers at a concert or at a club.

In the space below, design a poster to encourage young people to look after their hearing by avoiding listening to loud music.

Unit 11 Sound

Exercise 11.5 Range of hearing

In this exercise, you will interpret data concerning the different frequencies of sound which we can hear.

The frequency of a sound tells us the number of vibrations per second in a sound wave.

Frequency is measured in units called hertz (Hz). 1 Hz = 1 vibration per second.

High frequencies are measured in kilohertz (kHz).
1 kHz = 1000 Hz = 1000 vibrations per second.

The range of human hearing is from 20 Hz to 20 000 Hz.

1 What is 20 000 Hz in kHz? ....

2 Could a person with normal hearing hear a sound of 45 kHz? ....

As people get older, their range of hearing decreases. The graph shows how the highest frequency which can be heard decreases as someone gets older.

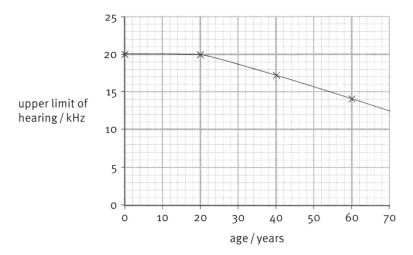

3 What is the highest audible frequency when a person is 60 years old?

....

4 At what age does the range of hearing start to decrease? ....

5 Could a person aged 40 hear a sound of frequency 15 kHz? ....

Mice can hear sounds with frequencies between 1 kHz and 70 kHz.

6 Are there frequencies which mice can hear but humans cannot? ....

7 Which frequencies can humans hear but mice cannot? ....

The picture above shows an experiment to find out the highest frequencies which students can hear.

8 On the picture, label the signal generator and the loudspeaker.

When the teacher turns the dial, the frequency of the sound from the loudspeaker increases. The students put their hands down when they can no longer hear the sound.

9 Some students have their hands up while others have put their hands down. What conclusion can you draw from this observation?

....

....

....

10 The teacher suspects that some students are not giving honest responses; they are keeping their hands up even when they can no longer hear the sound. How could he check if he is right?

....

....

....

Unit 12 Light

Exercise 12.1 Travelling light

In this exercise, you will use and interpret information about how light travels.

1 We can see objects that are luminous. They are sources of light.

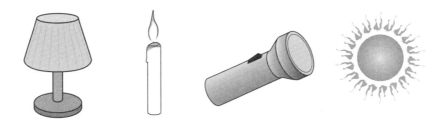

a Name the luminous objects shown above.

....

....

b Name some other luminous objects:

one in space ....

one in your home ....

one that is a living creature ....

c Are you a luminous or non-luminous object? ....

d Explain how a friend can see you on a sunny day.

....

....

....

....

2 How fast does light travel? It travels very fast indeed. Early scientists found it very hard to measure the speed of light. The picture shows how Galileo tried to measure the speed of light in the seventeenth century.

This method works fine for sound but not for light!

- His friend stood on a distant hill.
- Galileo flashed his lamp and started his clock at the same moment.
- When his friend saw the light, he flashed his lamp back towards Galileo.
- When Galileo saw the flash, he noted the time taken on his clock.

Unfortunately, this method didn't work. This was because the light travelled very quickly from one hill to the other. It took only a tiny fraction of a second. It took much longer for his friend to see the light and react to it, flashing his own lamp.

a This method would work quite well if Galileo wanted to measure the speed of sound. If his friend was 3000 m away, how long would the sound take to travel between the two hills? The speed of sound is about 300 m/s.

b Light travels one million times faster than sound. How long would light take to travel from one hill to the other?

....

c How quickly can you react when someone flashes a lamp? Suggest how you could find out an answer to this question.

....

....

....

....

....

....

....

....

....

....

Exercise 12.2 Shadows

In this exercise, you will use what you have learnt about how shadows form.

1 Shadows form when light is blocked. The picture below shows a scene on a sunny day. Your task is to show where there will be shadows on the ground.

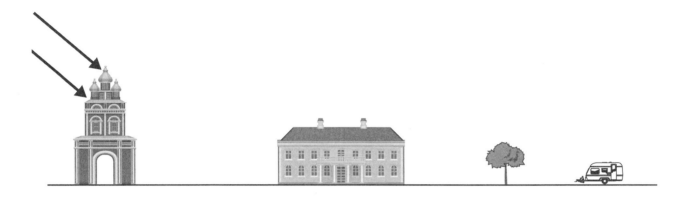

The Sun is shining. Two rays of sunlight are shown. They are parallel to each other.

Add to the picture by drawing more rays of light. Remember that they must all be parallel to each other.

Use a black pen or pencil to mark the areas on the ground where there will be shadows.

2 In the middle of the day, the Sun is much higher in the sky and shadows are much shorter. On the picture below, draw parallel rays of sunlight at midday and mark where the shadows will be.

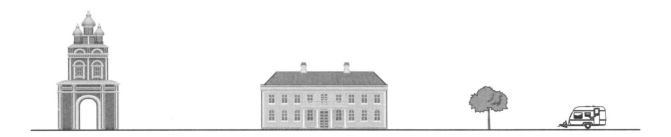

Unit 12 Light

3 When the astronomer Galileo first looked through a telescope at the Moon in 1609, he saw that its surface was covered in mountains and craters. He could see these because they were lit up by sunlight and they had very clear shadows.

Your task is to find some photographs or drawings of craters on the Moon.

Study them carefully and, in the space below, sketch a typical crater and label the shadows. Draw an arrow to show the direction of the sunlight which is lighting up the crater.

Exercise 12.3   Seeing by reflection

In this exercise, you will evaluate statements about how we see by reflected light.

We see things because light rays travel from them into our eyes. The picture shows a boy looking in a mirror. The girl can also see the boy.

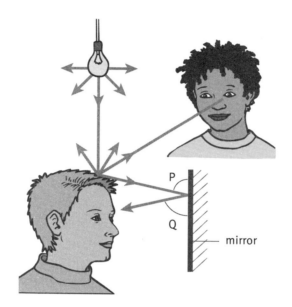

Study each sentence below.

- If the sentence is correct, put a tick (✔) at the end.
- If the sentence is incorrect, cross out the incorrect words and, in the space below, write words which will make the sentence correct.

1 The lamp is a non-luminous object.

....

2 Light from the lamp spreads out into the room.

....

3 Light rays travel from the girl's eyes to the boy's hair.

....

4 The boy can see an image of his hair in the mirror.

....

5 Angle **Q** is greater than Angle **P**.

....

6 The law of reflection allows us to predict the direction of a ray of light when it is reflected by a flat mirror.

....

Exercise 12.4   Refraction of light

In this exercise, you will apply what you have learnt about how light is refracted.

1 Complete the sentences below using the phrases in the box.

bends towards the normal.
passes from one material to another.
must be transparent.

a   If light is to pass through a material, the material ....

....

b   Refraction is the bending of light when it ....

....

c   When a ray of light passes from air into glass, it ....

....

2 Complete the diagrams to show how each light ray will travel.

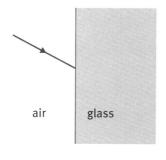

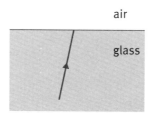

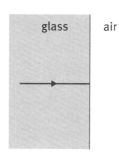

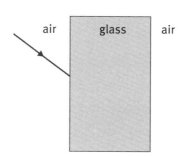

Unit 12 Light

Exercise 12.6　Coloured light

In this exercise, you will use what you have learnt about light and colour to devise questions for a quiz.

In each part of this exercise, you will be given some information. You will have to answer one question, based on the information (**a**). You will also have to devise two quiz questions of your own, and give the answers (**b** and **c**).

1 The diagram shows how a spectrum of white light can be produced, using a prism.

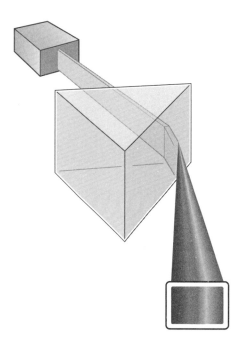

    a　What colour is at the opposite end of the spectrum to red?

        ....

    b　...

        ....

    c　...

        ....

2 The diagram shows what happens when different colours of light combine.
   This is colour addition.

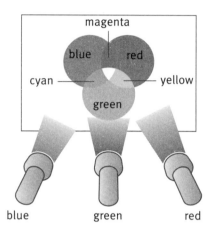

a   What two colours combine to give yellow light?

     ....

b   ....

     ....

c   ....

     ....

3 The diagram shows what happens when white light falls on a blue object. Blue light is reflected. This is colour subtraction.

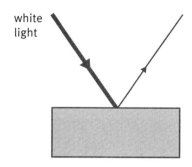

white
light

a What colours of light are absorbed when white light falls on a green object?

....

....

b ....

....

c ....

....

4 A red filter lets red and orange light pass through. It absorbs the other colours of light.

a White light shines through a red filter on to a blue car. What colour will

the car appear? ....

b ....

....

c ....

....

Exercise 13.1   Magnets and magnetic materials

> This exercise will help you to check that you know how different materials behave when you bring a magnet close to them.

1 Mohammed is testing different materials to discover which are magnetic.

   a Write a sentence to describe what he should do.

   ....

   ....

   ....

   b The table shows the items he tested. Indicate in the second column whether each item would be attracted by a bar magnet (tick) or not attracted (cross).

Item	Attracted (✓) or not attracted (✗)
copper coin	
steel paper clip	
aluminium foil tray	
plastic cup	
wooden stick	
iron nail	
water in a cup	

   c Name another item that **would be attracted** by a permanent magnet.

   ....

   d Name another item that **would not be attracted** by a permanent magnet.

   ....

2 The picture shows the corner of the door of a refrigerator.

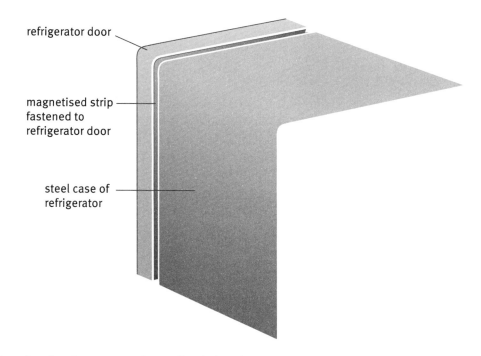

refrigerator door

magnetised strip
fastened to
refrigerator door

steel case of
refrigerator

Explain why the door stays shut after it has been closed.

....

....

....

....

Exercise 13.2   Magnetic forces, making magnets

> This exercise will test how well you understand what happens when magnets and magnetic materials are brought close together.

1 Nikita's teacher gives her some pieces of metal to test. They have been wrapped up so that Nikita cannot tell whether they are magnets or not.

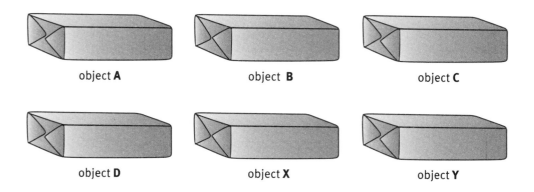

object **A**   object **B**   object **C**

object **D**   object **X**   object **Y**

a   Nikita brings objects **A** and **B** close together. The objects attract each other.

Nikita writes: 'Objects **A** and **B** are both permanent magnets, because they attract each other.'

Do you agree with Nikita? Explain your answer.

....

....

....

....

b   Nikita brings objects **C** and **D** together. The objects repel each other.

What can you say about objects **C** and **D**? Explain your answer.

....

....

....

....

c Nikita brings objects **X** and **Y** together. The objects neither attract nor repel.

Nikita writes: 'Neither **X** nor **Y** is a permanent magnet.'

Nikita might be right but she might be wrong. Explain how you would test her answer to see if she is correct.

....

....

....

....

....

....

....

2 Why does a piece of iron become magnetised when you stroke it with a permanent magnet?

Scientists imagine that a piece of iron is made up of many tiny regions called domains. Each domain behaves like a tiny magnet with its own magnetic field.

- In a piece of unmagnetised iron, the domains are all jumbled up. Their magnetic fields cancel each other out.
- When the iron is stroked with a magnet, each domain is attracted by the magnet. The domains all turn round so that they become lined up. Then all their magnetic fields add together to make a strong field.

a Look at the diagrams below. The arrows represent the magnetic domains.

Underneath the diagrams, add labels: **unmagnetised iron** and **magnetised iron**.

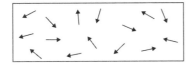

b The next diagram shows what happens when a bar magnet is cut in half.

Describe the result of cutting a bar magnet in half like this.

....

....

....

....

Exercise 13.3   Representing magnetic fields

This exercise will help you to understand how we represent magnetic fields using magnetic field lines.

1 The picture below shows the magnetic field around a bar magnet.

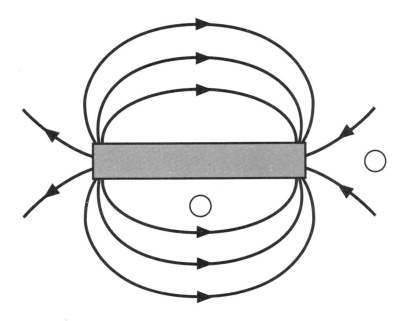

a On the diagram, label the north (N) and south (S) poles of the magnet.

b Explain how you know which is the north pole.

....

....

c The two circles on the diagram represent compasses. Draw the needle of each compass, showing how it will line up in the magnetic field of the magnet.

d Explain how you can tell from the diagram that the magnetic field is strongest close to the magnet's poles.

....

....

e   In the diagram below, you can see the outline of a bar magnet. Using a pencil, shade the area around the magnet to show how strong the magnetic field is.
  • Use dark shading to show where the field is strong.
  • Use light shading to show where the field is weak.

N	S

f   Give a reason why field lines are a better way of showing a magnetic field pattern than shading.

....

....

2 The diagram below shows two magnets.

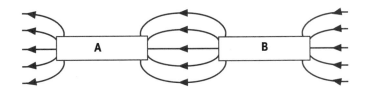

a On the diagram, label the north (N) and south (S) poles of each magnet.

b Are the magnets attracting or repelling each other? Explain how you know.

....

....

....

c Add force arrows to the diagram to show the force each magnet exerts on the other. Label the arrows '**force of A on B**' and '**force of B on A**'.

d Imagine that you could place a compass exactly half way between the two magnets. Add an arrow to the diagram to show how its needle would point.

Exercise 13.5   Magnets and electromagnets

This exercise will test your understanding of permanent magnets and electromagnets.

Each statement below is incorrect.

- Cross out the incorrect part of each statement.
- In the space below, write a correction so that the statement is correct.

1 A bar magnet has a north pole at one end and a west pole at the other.

....

2 The north pole of a magnet is attracted to the Earth's south pole.

....

3 A bar magnet needs an electricity supply to make it work.

....

4 The core of an electromagnet must be made of a non-magnetic material.

....

5 An electromagnet remains magnetised when the electric current in its coils is switched off.

....

6 Decreasing the current in an electromagnet will make its magnetic field stronger.

....

Exercise 13.6   Revising magnets and electromagnets

This exercise will test what you have learnt in this topic.

Here are some terms that you have learnt while studying magnetism.

magnetic field   **electromagnet**   **magnetic pole**   **magnetic field line**

ammeter   **core**   **compass**   **like poles**

1 The table below shows definitions of four of these terms. Write the terms in the spaces in the first column.

2 Now write the remaining four terms in the other spaces in the first column. Write a definition of each of these in the second column.

Term	Definition
	a permanent magnet which can turn freely in the Earth's magnetic field
	two north magnetic poles, or two south magnetic poles
	an instrument used to measure electric current
	a line drawn to show the direction of a magnetic field